Joel Sims

the Helper

What does it mean to be Spirit filled?

Unless otherwise indicated, all Scripture quotations are taken from the New American Standard Bible of the Bible.

Scripture quotations marked AMP are taken from the Amplified® Bible, Copyright © 1954, 1958, 1962, 1964, 1965, 1987 by The Lockman Foundation. Used by permission.

Scripture quotations marked MSG taken from The Message. Copyright © 1993, 1994, 1995, 1996, 2000, 2001, 2002. Used by permission of NavPress Publishing Group.

The Helper
ISBN 979-8-9892610-0-0
Copyright © 2023 by Joel Sims
Word of Life Church
5401 Lakeland Drive
Flowood, MS 39232

Printed in the United States of America. All rights reserved under International Copyright Law. Contents and/or cover may not be reproduced in whole or in part in any form without the express written consent of the Publisher.

Table *of* Contents

INTRODUCTION

Page 1

CHAPTER 1
THREE BAPTISMS

Page 7

CHAPTER 2
GOD'S GIFT TO HIS CHILDREN

Page 27

CHAPTER 3
SAME EXPERIENCE

Page 43

CHAPTER 4
WHY TONGUES

Page 51

CHAPTER 5
CONCLUSIONS

Page 69

INTRODUCTION

the Helper

I'm so excited you picked up this book. I pray it helps you understand the role the Holy Spirit wants to have in your life. I am honored to help be a guide, showing what life with Him can look like for you.

After initially receiving Jesus as our personal Lord and Savior and becoming a new creation in Christ, the greatest gift we could ever receive is the gift of being filled with the Holy Spirit. His reach and ability in our lives is so much greater than we can possibly comprehend. For many years, I have grown in my understanding of the role of the Holy Spirit in my own life. As I look at all that has taken place since I have been pastoring, I know beyond a shadow of a doubt, without the Holy Spirit leading and guiding me, none of what God has done through me would have been possible.

Referring to the Holy Spirit, Jesus told His disciples about some things that would unfold for them when He said, "And I will ask the Father, and He will give you another Helper, to be with you forever." (John 14:16 ESV) First, notice that the Holy Spirit is called "another Helper." God knew how much the disciples depended on Jesus, and He wasn't about to leave them helpless after Jesus left the earth. Also notice that the Scripture says, "to be with you forever." In other words, He, the Holy Spirit, hasn't left. He is still helping people all over the world today just like He did when He helped those in the early church.

I've been so blessed to have grown up in an environment where I always knew life with the Holy Spirit. It wasn't until I was in my teenage years that I realized the life experiences of so many people were different. I've encountered far too many Christians who were resistant and fearful of the Holy Spirit for various reasons. Some have been taught that the Holy Spirit is not for today while others have been taught incorrect doctrine regarding the Holy Spirit. Some doctrines place a religious stigma on being filled with the Holy Spirit, leaving an impression that it is weird, strange, and mystical, but nothing could be further from the truth.

Throughout the Bible, we find so many instances where the Holy Spirit's involvement brought about transformation, help, direction, revival, healing, and revelation. Guess what? He hasn't changed. I have witnessed His power transforming ordinary people into extraordinary people. I can't begin to count the testimonies of people whose lives have been totally transformed by His power. The amazing thing about His power is that it is available to every single follower of Christ who desires the infilling of the Holy Spirit and makes the decision to receive Him.

Contained in the pages of this book, you will find the answers to turn your life into a life marked by destiny – an extraordinary life, a supernatural life. Come with me on this journey as we learn about the three baptisms that transform us into the men and women that God desires us to become.

You will see that you have an eternal home in Heaven available to you. Have you been baptized into Christ, securing your eternal home? While obtaining your eternal salvation is magnificent, you will also see that the Holy Spirit wants to be your personal Helper, aiding and guiding you into the most spectacular life you could ever imagine. Do you know Him that way?

Additionally, you will come to see the transformative power of speaking by the Holy Spirit. Do you have that gift? One day while I was preparing to deliver a message to my congregation regarding this gift, I told the Lord that I did not want to "over-promise" the impact of this gift. Emphatically, He assured me that there is absolutely no way to "over-promise" the difference this gift will make in the life of a believer.

If you're ready to see your life soar to new heights and become the absolute best version of yourself, then the truths you're about to read will take you there. My prayer for you as you read through the pages of this book, is that you will come to understand the truth about the Holy Spirit, and He will become the Helper to you that God promised He would be.

CHAPTER

1

THREE
BAPTISMS

Throughout the New Testament, we find three different baptisms mentioned. Each of these baptisms mark a pivotal moment in the life of the Christian. It is important to recognize there is an order in which these baptisms take place. As you gain a better understanding of each, you will come to see and understand the work of the Holy Spirit in your own life.

The first baptism is when we are baptized into Christ by the Holy Spirit. This is a spiritual baptism and takes place when you give your life to the Lord, asking Jesus to be your personal Lord and Savior. At this very moment, you and Christ become one. Something happens on the inside of you, and your spirit is now alive unto God. You may ask, how does the Holy Spirit baptize us into Christ?

The role of the Holy Spirit in our lives is something that people often overlook. If you stop and trace the steps you've taken throughout your life, you will see His involvement. When Jesus was speaking to His disciples in John 15, He pointed out one of the purposes for the Holy Spirit in our life.

> **John 15:26 KJV,** *But when the Comforter is come, whom I will send unto you from the Father, even the Spirit of truth, which proceedeth from the Father, he shall testify of me;*

In this verse, Jesus explained to His disciples that one of the roles of the Holy Spirit is to testify about Himself – Jesus. In other words, the Holy Spirit will always point people to Jesus. Regardless of who you are, if you are born again, you can be assured that the Holy Spirit has been active in your life. The small nudge that touched your heart one day and led you to receive Jesus was the Holy Spirit. Whether you received Jesus by responding to an altar call in a church service, watching a television broadcast, kneeling by yourself in your home, or any other way, it was the Holy Spirit that steered you towards Jesus. He is always trying to awaken people to their need for Jesus.

In I Corinthians 12, the Apostle Paul is explaining the ways of Christ, and he likens the body of Christ to our physical bodies.

> **I Corinthians 12:12 NASB 1995,** ***For even as the body is one and yet hath many members, and all the members of the body, though they are many, are one body, so also is Christ.***

In other words, your physical body is made up of your nose, your eyes, your mouth, your fingers, and every other part of your body. In the same way, the entire body of Christ is made up of many members (believers), and all the members are part of the same body of Christ.

Now, watch how He builds the body in the next verse.

> **I Corinthians 12:13 NASB 1995,** ***For by one Spirit we were all baptized into one body, whether Jews or Greeks, whether slaves or free, and we were all made to drink of one Spirit.***

Notice the terminology "for by one Spirit we were all baptized into one body." The body that the scripture is referring to is the body of Jesus, and He says, it's the Spirit who took you into that body. If you're born again today, meaning you have asked Jesus Christ to be your Lord and Savior, you were baptized by the Holy Spirit into Christ Jesus. Now you're part of the family of God, which means you are part of the body of Christ.

Reflecting on my own life, when I experienced this baptism, I couldn't remember the first moment that I received Jesus as my Lord and Savior, but I do remember a transformative moment in my life as a teenager. I was raised in a pastor's home, so going to church was completely normal for me. As a result, I was accustomed to seeing people give their hearts to Jesus. I can remember raising my hand multiple times to receive Jesus while I was still a child during children's church puppet ministry. However, in my teenage years, I began to drift away into some things in which I shouldn't have become involved. During that season, going to church became a "have to." Reading my Bible became a "have to." The things that I was taught to do growing up all became "have to's" in my life. I was still attending summer camps and church services, so seeds were being sown into me, but my desire to live for the Lord had waned.

One day when I was 17 years old, I was lying on my bed, and I couldn't sleep. I sensed the Holy Spirit – not in a "spooky" way, but I just knew He was present. He began dealing with my heart about my need to surrender to Jesus. There were no flashing lights or heavenly appearances; it was just a specific thought that came to me that I needed to surrender to Jesus. So, there, all by myself, I knelt by my bedside and said, "Dear Lord Jesus, take my life. I offer it to you as a living sacrifice and I give it to you."

It was at that moment that I felt like I had been baptized into Christ. Suddenly, all my "have to's" turned into "want to's." No longer did I feel like I had to go to church; I WANTED to go to church. No longer did I feel like I had to read my Bible; I WANTED to read my Bible. It was such a heart change that I no longer wanted to be around the people with whom I had been spending time because I no longer wanted to be involved in those things that were wrong. In fact, I got a job at a local ice cream shop, Bop's on County Line Road, and asked my supervisor specifically if I could work on Friday and Saturday nights just so I would be too busy to participate in the things that I had been doing on weekends.

My heart had completely changed, and as a result my desires changed. Ezekiel 36:26 NLT says, "...I will take out your stony, stubborn heart and give you a tender, responsive heart." This is symbolic of being baptized into Christ, and this is exactly what happened to me that day. Literally, I was changed from the inside out. Now, this doesn't mean that from the age of 17 until today I have lived perfectly or that my life has been free of problems. It simply means on that day I began to have a sincere desire to surrender my life to Christ. Through the years there have been areas of my life that I know were not completely surrendered, but I wanted them to be. Now, because I have been baptized into Christ, I have continued to surrender those areas to Him.

Water Baptism

The second baptism mentioned in scripture occurs when a believer in Christ is baptized in water. This is simply an outward expression of what has taken place on the inside of a believer in Christ Jesus, and it is an opportunity for you to make public your faith in Jesus.

> **Matthew 28:19 ESV,** *Go therefore and make disciples of all nations, baptizing them in the name of the Father and the Son and the Holy Spirit.*

Again, this is water baptism, and we see this demonstrated throughout Scripture. Jesus and many of His followers were water baptized. There is a story found in Acts 8:26-39 that demonstrates the need for water baptism after someone has been baptized into Christ.

At the time, there was a great spiritual revival taking place. Phillip, the evangelist, was experiencing great miracles from God in his ministry. One day, as he was praying, God showed him that he needed to change the direction he was going on his journey. By the leading of the Holy Spirit, he came upon a certain eunuch from Ethiopia that happened to be a man of great prominence. This meeting would, for example, be equivalent to you or me coming upon the Secretary of State of the United States of America.

As he came upon this eunuch, Philip found him by the river reading a passage from the prophet Isaiah which referred to the Lamb who was to be slain yet opened not His mouth. When Philip saw him, the Holy Spirit said, "That's why I sent you." Philip approached him and asked, "Do you understand these scriptures?" The eunuch told Phillip that he did not understand to whom this scripture was referring. Notice Philip's response to the eunuch.

> **Acts 8:35 NASB 1995, *Then Philip opened his mouth and beginning from this Scripture, he preached Jesus unto him.***

I love this! Philip was not intimidated by the prominence of this man; he simply preached Jesus to him, which led to two baptisms, one right after the other.

Acts 8:36-38.
As they went along the road they came to some water; and the eunuch said, "Look! Water! What prevents me from being baptized?

And Philip said,
"If you believe with all your heart, you may." And he answered and said, "I believe that Jesus Christ is the Son of God."

And he ordered the chariot to stop; and they both went down into the water, Philip as well as the eunuch, and he baptized him

Right there at the same moment the eunuch was baptized into Christ and baptized in water. Both of these baptisms were orchestrated by the Holy Spirit.

The spiritual baptism into Jesus gives you new life. Water baptism publicly demonstrates to the world your faith in Christ and your new attitude and commitment. With our new attitude we express, "I am not ashamed of the gospel of Jesus Christ! I don't want to be just a light that is shining but hidden under a bushel. I want to be public with my faith so everyone can see and know that I belong to God, and I am not ashamed of the good news of Christ!"

Not only does going public with your faith by being water baptized help others because they can see what Jesus has done in your life, it also helps you. It seals something in your heart. Water baptism is an outward physical sign of an inward work that is designed by God to give you a new attitude and strength of commitment to God.

Baptism in the Holy Spirit

The third baptism mentioned in scripture happens when a person is baptized by the Holy Spirit. The purpose of this baptism is to fill one's life with power. It will alter your vision so you can see things through the lens of God. Far too many Christians are content with only being baptized into Christ and being water baptized, and they miss the third baptism, the baptism of the Holy Spirit. The baptism of the Holy Spirit is far too special and beneficial for a believer and disciple of Christ to ignore. Let us investigate several passages of scripture so you can see how vital this baptism is for your life.

In Matthew 3 we see where John the Baptist was baptizing people in water, and he began telling people about who and what was to come.

> **Matthew 3:11 NASB 1995,** *As for me, I baptize you with water for repentance, but He who is coming after me is mightier than I, and I am not fit to remove his sandals; He will baptize you with the Holy Spirit and fire.*

Now let's look at Acts 1 where Jesus was gathered with His disciples. At this time, Jesus had already been to the cross and risen from the dead, and He had been with His disciples 40 days, encouraging them concerning the kingdom of God. Notice what Jesus highlights to His disciples.

> **Acts 1:4-8 NASB 1995,** *Gathering them together, He commanded them not to leave Jerusalem, but to wait for what the Father had promised, "Which," He said, "you heard of from me;*

For John baptized with water, but you will be baptized with the Holy Spirit not many days from now."

So when they had come together, they were asking Him, saying, "Lord, is it at this time You are restoring the kingdom to Israel?"

He said to them, "It is not for you to know times which the Father has fixed by His own authority but you will receive power when the Holy Spirit has come upon you and you will be witnesses both in Jerusalem and in Judea and in Samaria, even to the remote parts of the earth.

Here He told His disciples that there's another baptism. It is a baptism by the Holy Spirit, and it's a baptism that will give you **power.** The water baptism was a cleansing baptism, but this baptism by the Holy Spirit will give you power to live out who you have become in Christ.

Notice in the fourth verse Jesus commanded His disciples to not leave Jerusalem until they had received that baptism (the baptism of the Holy Spirit) because Jesus knew the difference it would make in their lives. He also knew that they would need the power of the Holy Spirit in order to be effective witnesses for Him. See how things transpired according to the following verses in Acts 2.

> **Acts 2:1-4 NASB 1995,** *When the day of Pentecost had come, they were all together in one place.*
>
> *And suddenly there came from heaven a noise like a violent rushing wind, and it filled the whole house where they were sitting.*
>
> *And there appeared unto them, tongues as of fire, distributing themselves, and they rested on each one of them.*

And they were all filled with the Holy Spirit and began to speak with other tongues, as the Spirit was giving them utterance.

Here we see that God came and filled the whole house, and there appeared unto them tongues as of fire, resting upon each one of them. Some people have surmised and argued that this supernatural experience was just for the original disciples (less Judas Iscariot), but this passage says that they were ALL filled. This included every man, woman, boy, and girl who was in that room. Now take a look at Peter's explanation of what was taking place.

Acts 2:14-18 (NASB 1995), But Peter, taking his stand with the eleven, raised his voice and declared to them: "Men of Judea and all you who live in Jerusalem, let this be known to you and give heed to my words.

For these men are not drunk, as you suppose, for it is only the third hour of the day;

But this is what was spoken of through the prophet Joel:

And it shall be in the last days, God says,

That I will pour forth of My Spirit on all mankind; And your sons and your daughters shall prophesy, and your young men shall see visions, and your old men shall dream dreams;

Even on My bondslaves, both men and women, I will in those days pour forth of My Spirit and they shall prophesy.

We can see in this passage how this baptism was not meant for only a select few in the early days of the church. First of all, this baptism of the Holy Spirit was prophesied long before this outpouring was recorded in the book of Acts. Additionally, He included your sons, your daughters, old men, young men, bond slaves, and women. There was not a gender, age group, or class of people left out of this special gift because Jesus knew that every Christian would need power in life.

As long as I can remember, I have been around the Holy Spirit-filled life. I was raised by Spirit-filled parents, faithfully attended a Spirit-filled church, and was surrounded by a Spirit-filled extended family. Almost everyone I knew was Spirit-filled, but as I became older and talked with friends, I realized that this was not the case for many people. Some of my friends even thought the baptism of the Holy Spirit was strange.

When my father passed away I was 17 years old. It was at that time I really saw the benefit of this power. I was broken, angry, and sorrowful. I needed God's power in my life like never before. Over time, He began to fix me and rebuild me. He did it through this baptism of fire. One night, while I was attending Bible school, I was in the coffee shop where I worked. On this particular night, there were a few of us getting ready to close down, and suddenly, God's Spirit filled the entire coffee shop. Everyone there was immediately filled with God's Holy Spirit. I had never seen or experienced anything like it, and although I had heard of things like this happening to others, this was the only time in my life it happened. We all hit the floor praying in the Spirit in other tongues. All at once, God became so very real to each of us.

As a result, that event started a prayer movement. We would get together daily and spend hours praying and singing in the Holy Spirit. It was so beautiful, and we experienced all you could ever want from the Lord. As I gave myself to this season of prayer, it began to give me power and strength in a way that God was able to heal me from past hurt and pain and into a miraculous life.

Because of that moment in the coffee shop, when I was baptized by the Holy Spirit, where I sought after all that God had for me in that baptism, I am a free man today. I am free from sorrow and hurt. I have peace and joy in my life that are beyond me and my every expectation.

Being filled with the Spirit of God produces a supernatural edge and aspect to your life that can become a reality by no other way. It creates vision within you so that you can see through the lens of God. You can see beyond moments of discomfort and pain and know that God's not leaving you in that place.

In the Old Testament, we see types and shadows of God's Spirit coming upon people where, for example, a king is anointed with oil. When the prophet, Samuel, anointed King Saul with oil, he was changed into another man. People looked at him and said, "Who is that?" (I Samuel 10:6-11) When David was anointed with oil by Samuel, the Bible says that the spirit of the Lord came upon him from that day forward. (I Samuel 16:13) Not long after that when David showed up at the battlefield and accepted the challenge of going up against Goliath, his own brothers stated, "Who do you think you are?" The anointing on David's life caused him to see Goliath through the lens of God. He didn't see Goliath as an obstacle or someone to be feared. David saw Goliath as someone or something that was standing in the way of God. By the power of the Spirit of God that was upon him, David knew he could defeat Goliath. (I Samuel 17:20-50)

This is exactly what happened to me when I was baptized by the Holy Spirit. I was turned into another man, and the power of God began to operate in my life like never before.

When Others Cast Doubt

There will be people who claim to have received the baptism of the Holy Spirit who may not demonstrate this power and strength to which I'm referring. Or, perhaps they cast doubt on this truth because after having experienced it once, they just don't see any difference that being filled with the Holy Spirit has made in their life. Let's look at what the Apostle Paul says about being filled with the Holy Spirit.

> **Ephesians 5:18 KJV,** *And be not drunk with wine, wherein is excess; but be filled with the Spirit;*

When you think of being drunk with wine, you don't drink wine, get drunk, and stay drunk forever. You must consistently drink wine if one desires to consistently stay drunk. When you're drunk, that alcohol is in control of you, and you act differently. You behave differently.

God wants us to know that this is what the Holy Spirit is like, but in a blessed way. It's not enough to have one experience of being filled with the Holy Spirit. If you want to stay full, you must continue to drink of His Spirit because when you drink of God's Spirit, you become more like Him. Suddenly, the fruit of the Spirit begins to flow out of you. Instead of reacting like you have previously, in your own flesh and mind, what comes out of you is love, joy, peace, patience, kindness, gentleness, meekness, and self-control. This is the Holy Spirit breaking forth out of you because you are filled with Him.

This third baptism will set your life apart in so many ways, and you will come to see just how amazing this gift from God the Father is to you.

CHAPTER

2

GOD'S GIFT
to HIS CHILDREN

Now that we have established what the baptism of the Holy Spirit is, let's look at some scriptures to learn more about the Holy Spirit and His role in our lives. One truth that you will see demonstrated and revealed time and time again is this, Jesus is God's gift to the world. The Holy Spirit is God's gift to His children. Jesus is an amazing gift! But once you have received Him, God is not finished giving to you. He still wants you to receive the special gift of the baptism of the Holy Spirit.

In the first chapter of the book of Acts, we find Jesus had gathered with His disciples telling them, "You wait here until the Holy Spirit comes upon you because you're going to need Him. Don't even attempt to do life without Him." As you know, those believers received and acted upon Jesus' command. Their lives were radically changed for the better when they received the gift of the Holy Spirit. This then became their mode of living. After sharing the gift of Jesus to unbelievers, they followed that message by sharing the gift of the Holy Spirit to the people once they became Christians.

Notice what Jesus said about the Holy Spirit in John 14.

> **John 14:16-17a NASB 1995,** ***I will ask the Father, and He will give you another Helper, that He may be with you forever;***

That is the Spirit of truth, whom the world cannot receive...

According to this scripture, the world cannot receive the Holy Spirit, which is the Spirit of truth. Why is that? Because the Holy Spirit is God's gift to His children. The world must first receive Jesus as their gift from God. When a person receives Jesus, they are born of the Spirit. However, once a person is filled with the Spirit, they are filled with the very Spirit by whom they were born. Now look at the rest of this passage.

> **John 14:17 NASB 1995,** *That is the Spirit of truth, whom the world cannot receive, because it does not see Him or know Him, but you know Him because He abides with you and will be in you.*

In this passage, Jesus is talking to His followers, and He is letting them know that after a person becomes a follower of Jesus, that is when they can be filled with the Holy Spirit.

In Mark chapter 2 Jesus gives another example of this when He says,

> **Mark 2:22 NASB 1995,** *No one puts new wine into old wineskins; otherwise the*

> ***wine will burst the skins, and the wine is lost and the skins as well; but one puts new wine into fresh wineskins.***

In other words, Jesus is saying that before He puts in the new wine, He must first give a person a fresh wineskin. This is a type and shadow of being born again, and then being filled with the Holy Spirit.

When you are born again, old things have passed away, and all things have become new. (2 Corinthians 5:17) This is the new wineskin of which Jesus was referring. You were not given that new wineskin to let sit idly, just to talk about it and do nothing. He gave you a new wineskin so He could pour into you some new wine!

We see evidence of this in Acts 8. There was much persecution taking place in the early church, mainly by Saul of Tarsus who later became the Apostle Paul. In this particular instance, Saul came to the church at Jerusalem, and began to brutally oppress the believers in Christ. Some were beaten, some were dragged away, and others were stoned and killed. This persecution by Saul and others did not cause the believers in Christ to cease worshiping God. The persecution actually caused the church to expand. As people fled Jerusalem, they went to other cities to preach the Gospel of Jesus.

In these scripture verses we see evidence of many people coming to Jesus. Jesus was being preached by Philip with the gospel of power. It wasn't just, "Come listen to me talk about who Jesus is." Rather, it was, "Let me show you who Jesus is! Let me show you His love, His power, and His saving nature for you!"

As a result, the presence of God was manifested. God's powerful display arrested the attention of the people in ways that they could not deny. They couldn't argue with the fact that a previously lame man was now running, leaping, and praising God. As a result of seeing the Gospel lived out in power, the people desired what God desired for them!

> Acts 8:12-13 NASB 1995, *But when they believed Philip preaching the good news about the kingdom of God and the name of Jesus Christ, they were being baptized, men and women alike.*
>
> *Even Simon himself believed; and after being baptized, he continued on with Philip, and as he observed signs and great miracles taking place, he was constantly amazed.*

We can see in these verses that the people were not only receiving Jesus, they were being baptized

Acts 8:4-8 NASB 1995,
Therefore, those who had been scattered went about preaching the word.

Philip went down to the city of Samaria and began proclaiming Christ to them.

The crowds with one accord were giving attention to what was said by Philip, as they heard and saw the signs which he was performing.

For in the case of many who had unclean spirits, they were coming out of them shouting with a loud voice; and many who had been paralyzed and lame were healed.

So there was much rejoicing in that city.

in water and publicly announcing their faith to the world. Let's see what happens next.

> Acts 8:14-17 NASB 1995, *Now when the apostles in Jerusalem heard that Samaria had received the Word of God, they sent them Peter and John,*
>
> *Who came down and prayed for them that they might receive the Holy Spirit.*
>
> *For He had not fallen upon any of them; they had simply been baptized in the name of the Lord Jesus.*
>
> *Then they began laying their hands on them, and they were receiving the Holy Spirit.*

The church in Samaria had not been serving God, and when the Word of God was preached to them, they received it, and they were baptized with water. Then, the very next thing that was presented to them was the infilling of the Holy Spirit. Unlike today, when a Sunday school class or scriptural teachings are frequently the recommended next steps for a new convert to Christ, the early church presented being filled with the Holy Spirit.

Once again, the early church knew that this infilling of the Holy Spirit should be received as soon as possible. They never hesitated to ask someone who had just received Jesus as their Lord if they had also received the Holy Spirit. Guess what? Neither should we.

The early church represents the kind of church that everyone should desire. It was a church filled with power, a church with radical generosity, a church that joyfully lived out its faith through righteous deeds. The Spirit of God moved mightily and freely in the early church, so much so, that the buildings where the early Christians met literally shook from the power of God. (Acts 4:31) Miracles, signs, and wonders were the norm in the early church. Do you know why? Because it was a Spirit-filled church. They unashamedly asked everyone who believed, "Have you received the Holy Spirit since you believed?" They had experienced precisely what Acts 1:8 says, "But you will receive power when the Holy Spirit has come upon you; and you shall be My witnesses…"

God's plan regarding the Holy Spirit has never changed. He never intended Christians to take the gift of the Holy Spirit lightly or to regard the Holy Spirit as optional. As soon as a person is born again, God desires them to be filled with His Holy Spirit so their life will be infused with His power.

I was blessed to have grown up with this truth my entire life. The truth of being baptized by the Holy Spirit is strong in my heart because I know that experience is absolutely life-changing. Over the course of my pastoral ministry, I have observed countless numbers of people are fearful of the Holy Spirit, and that absolutely breaks my heart. I have actually wept over the way religion has made the Holy Spirit seem to be someone He is not. Satan, the enemy, has placed a stigma on the Holy Spirit, making Him seem weird, strange, and someone who cannot be understood. In the Bible we see the complete opposite. The Holy Spirit is revealed as a perfect gentleman, in total harmony with God the Father and God the Son.

The Holy Spirit is the God of peace. The first instance we find of the Holy Spirit in the scriptures is found in Genesis chapter one. There was darkness and chaos, but the Holy Spirit was hovering over the waters. (Genesis 1:2) As God began to speak and the Spirit began to move, what was out of order came into order. What was dark became light. What was ugly became beautiful.

We should all ask ourselves the following questions, "How much of my life could use this kind of transformation?" "How much of my life is out of order?" "How much of my life sits in darkness?" "How much of my life is not the beauty that I desire to see?"

In God's great love and infinite wisdom, He placed the Holy Spirit in the earth and offered us this amazing gift of being filled with Him. Once we're filled with Him, we are given a heavenly language called the gift of other tongues in order to communicate with God. While we're praying, the Holy Spirit is moving, taking what is out of order and putting it into order. Taking what is dark and bringing it into light. Taking what is ugly and making it beautiful. This is the Person and character of the Holy Spirit.

The Dove

In Luke 3 we find the time when Jesus along with other people were baptized with water. Something significant took place, demonstrating the Holy Spirit's nature.

> Luke 3:21-22 NASB 1995, *Now when all the people were baptized, Jesus was also baptized, and while He was praying, heaven was opened,*
>
> *And the Holy Spirit descended upon Him in bodily form like a dove, and a voice came out of heaven, "You are My Beloved Son, in You I am well-pleased."*

When the Holy Spirit descended upon Jesus, we see the Holy Spirit was in the form of a dove. Why, of all the animals that could have been chosen, do you think a dove was used? Universally, the dove is a symbol of peace, and this is precisely how the Holy Spirit comes to us. He always comes to us as peace. He'll never harm you, confuse you, or intimidate you. He's not someone to be feared, and He's not going to cause you to have an experience that would make you nervous. He comes to you in the form of peace. In Matthew 10:16, Jesus even makes reference to being harmless as a dove.

God knew the enemy would try to discredit the work of the Holy Spirit in the lives of believers. As a result, God demonstrated the character and nature of the Holy Spirit by using a dove. In Matthew 7:9-11, Jesus taught about the Holy Spirit. He said,

> **Matthew 7:9-11 NASB 1995** *What man is there among you who, when his son asks for a loaf, will give him a stone?*
>
> *Or if he asks for a fish, he will not give him a snake, will he?*
>
> *If you then, being evil, know how to give good gifts to your children, how much more will your Father who is in heaven give what is good to those who ask Him!*

In other words, Jesus said if you ask the Father for the Holy Spirit, He's not going to give you something to frighten you. He wants to eliminate all fear associated with the Holy Spirit because in truth, He comes as peace.

One day as I was meditating on these things, I began searching for the first place that a dove was spoken of in the Bible. It is found in the book of Genesis when Noah sent the dove out of the ark. The world had just been flooded by water. When Noah sent out a dove, it came back with an olive branch. (Genesis 8:11)

The olive branch was a type and shadow of the oil of the Holy Spirit that comes with the power of God. Of all the things that the dove could have returned with, he brought back the very thing that grows the fruit, which when pressed, produces oil that is used to anoint men and women of God. This story is symbolic of entering a new place, which was actually the old place that had been washed clean by the power of God. Although the earth had been washed (baptized) by the power of God, there was still a necessary endowment of power from on high by the person of the Holy Spirit.

I have a good friend who related a personal story to me years ago that demonstrates the power of walking with the Holy Spirit. He and his wife own a very successful business, and like many people, he got busy with work and was occupied with the responsibilities of owning a thriving business. As a result, his attention was focused more on the natural things he was dealing with instead of spiritual things. His heart knew it, and he knew he needed to make an adjustment.

One morning as he was making coffee, with a sincere heart, he said, "Thank you Lord. Thank you for this life. Thank you, Lord." As soon as he said that, the Spirit of God came on him, and he began to pray in the Spirit. He went over to a nearby ottoman and knelt beside it as he continued praying in the Spirit. As he was praying, his wife came up behind him, put her hands on him, and began praying in the Spirit as well.

As they were both praying, he saw a vision of himself bound by a heavy chain that resembled one that you would see coming off a big cruise ship. It was wrapped around him, and he couldn't move. He saw something hanging on the chain. It was something that he had dealt with since he was a young boy but had never been able to completely surrender it to the Lord. He would go through seasons where he would want to and try to surrender it, but he was unable to break free from it.

During this time of prayer, he became aware that if the bondage represented by the chain wasn't broken over his life, that bondage would spread throughout his family. As they continued to pray in the Spirit, he saw this chain break, and he knew instantly he was free. From that moment on, he has never wrestled with that bondage since.

When I think about that olive branch, I think about stories like this. Although this man is a devout

Christian man, there was still something that held him in bondage. When the Holy Spirit got involved and helped him through prayer, there was new life waiting for him. Never again has he struggled with that aspect of his life because the Holy Spirit brought the anointing that was needed to destroy that yoke. (Isaiah 10:27) This is an example of the power of the Holy Spirit!

Everyone has certain things in their lives that they deal with, and it's by the power of the Holy Spirit that yokes will be destroyed and new life can come. The olive branch is symbolic of this new life. It was proof to Noah and his family that something was growing again, that an old season had ended and a new one had begun. Although they were confined in the ark, they were about to be released to a new life.

Let this be the moment when you realize, through the power of the Holy Spirit, something is growing again for you. There is a new season awaiting you when you are filled with the Holy Spirit and fully yielded to Him. Things that may have trapped you or tripped you up in the past can no longer hold you captive when, by the power of the Holy Spirit, you break free of those chains.

Praying Families

Another aspect to the story of my friend is well worth noting. My friend had a wife who joined him in prayer. She didn't even know what he was praying about, but she took the opportunity to join him as he prayed. It is a beautiful thing when both a husband and wife are Spirit-filled, and they can believe God together in prayer. The spiritual dynamics of a Spirit-filled family contain power that is not of this world.

I'm very thankful for the generations that went before me and raised me in this Spirit-filled life, but the work is not finished. We need a new generation of praying mothers and fathers, of praying husbands and wives, to pick up the Holy Spirit prayer mantle so it's not lost to future generations. We need more people moving in the power of the Holy Spirit to set the captives free, including themselves and their families.

When you receive the priceless gift of the Holy Spirit from God the Father, you enter into what can be the most beautiful and powerful life you could ever imagine. He wants you to know Him, be led by Him, and be empowered by Him. God has a perfect plan for you, and with the Holy Spirit as your Helper, you can fulfill all God has for you!

CHAPTER

3

SAME EXPERIENCE

The evidence throughout the Word of God regarding the need for the Holy Spirit in the life of believers far outweighs the somewhat popular belief and teaching that the Holy Spirit is no longer relevant. Today, more than ever, we need His power operating in our lives. One of the problems I currently see in the church is that we have asked people to live a Jesus type of life without giving them the power that Jesus had. Why would we do that when the same power is available to the church?

After Jesus was baptized by John the Baptist, and the Holy Spirit came upon Him, Jesus was led by the Spirit into the wilderness. It was during this time that Jesus fasted 40 days and nights. At the end of this 40 day fast, Jesus demonstrated the empowerment of the Holy Spirit by resisting Satan's temptations one after another. (Matthew 4:2-11) By this, He showed us an example of what happens to us when the Holy Spirit comes upon our lives and we yield to the Holy Spirit. It puts us in greater control of our flesh and empowers us to resist temptations when they come.

I see far too many Christians today struggling, living a life of weakness and frustration. This can change when we yield to the power of the Holy Spirit within us. Let's take a look at three different instances in the New Testament where we see what happens when a person receives this gift and is filled with the Holy Spirit.

In Acts 19, the Apostle Paul was passing through the upper country and came to Ephesus where he found some disciples. Disciples are more than just believers. They truly want to do life the Jesus way. They ask questions like, "How does Jesus want me to handle my money?" "How does Jesus want me to treat an enemy?" They are people who are genuinely trying to do what God wants them to do. Notice what happens when Paul comes into contact with these disciples.

> **Acts 19:2-7 NASB,** *He said to them, "Did you receive the Holy Spirit when you believed? And they said to him, "No, we have not even heard whether there is a Holy Spirit."*
>
> *And he said, "Into what then were you baptized? And they said, "Into John's baptism.*
>
> *Paul said, "John baptized with the baptism of repentance, telling the people to believe in Him who was coming after him, that is, in Jesus."*

> *When they heard this, they were baptized in the name of the Lord Jesus.*
>
> *And when Paul had laid his hands upon them, the Holy Spirit came on them, and they began speaking with tongues and prophesying.*
>
> *There were about twelve men.*

Here we see a separate experience outside of salvation called the infilling of the Holy Spirit. Once Paul established that they were Christians, Paul's immediate reaction was to ask, "Have you received the Holy Spirit since you believed?" Why is that? Because the disciples had experienced how transformative receiving the Holy Spirit had been in their own lives. Besides that, receiving the Holy Spirit was the main directive that Jesus gave His early church. (Acts 1:4-8) Jesus knew how vital being filled with the Holy Spirit was in order to fulfill their mission.

Notice what happened to these disciples as a result of being filled with the Holy Spirit, "...they began speaking with tongues and prophesying." (Acts 19:6) Speaking in tongues is something that many people are confused or uncertain about because they don't understand it. We will dig deeper into this later in this book, but for now I'll explain it this way. Have you ever been in a setting where people are conversing in a foreign language? Although you are not fluent in that language, nor do you understand it, it is still beautiful to hear. There is no doubt in your mind that they know perfectly well what is being communicated between themselves because they are speaking their own language. It is not strange that their language sounds different from yours.

Heaven and God's heavenly realm has its own language too, and it's called other tongues. When you are filled with the Holy Spirit, you are given the opportunity to speak in that heavenly language. It is a language that can only be shared between you and God. It is truly a beautiful language.

In Acts 10, we find another time when being filled with the Holy Spirit was presented to a man by the name of Cornelius. Up until this time, the Gospel was preached only to the Jews. Cornelius was a devout man who desired to live right, but he was a Gentile. One day while praying, God met him in an extraordinary way by telling Cornelius that salvation was about to come to his house. God told him to gather up his entire family and go look for a man named Peter.

While this was going on, Peter was praying on the roof of his house. While praying, Peter had a vision, letting him know that salvation was not just for the Jews. Peter saw that salvation was for the whole world. God showed him that someone was about to come to him, seeking salvation.

By the guidance of the Holy Spirit, these two men met, and Peter began teaching Cornelius and his family about Jesus. It is amazing to see what happened when Peter was ministering to them.

> **Acts 10:44-46 KJV,** ***While Peter yet spoke these words, the Holy Ghost fell on all them which heard the Word.***
>
> ***And they of the circumcision which believed were astonished, as many as came with Peter, because that on the Gentiles also was poured out the gift of the Holy Spirit.***
>
> ***For they heard them speak with tongues, and magnify God...***

Did you notice what the scripture reports here? People were astonished because the Holy Spirit was poured out on Gentiles. Why is that? Because of what we see in verse 46 "...for they heard them speak with tongues, and magnify God." They spoke in other tongues just like the believers in Acts 19 did. This was an outward demonstration of being filled with the Holy Spirit. Once again, we see here that when we receive God's gift of the Holy Spirit, we can begin speaking in other tongues.

The third instance occurred on the day of Pentecost when the Holy Spirit was poured out for the first time on the children of God. We find this momentous event in Acts 2.

> **Acts 2:1-4 KJV,** *And when the day of Pentecost was fully come, they were all with one accord in one place.*
>
> *And suddenly there came a sound from heaven as a rushing mighty wind, and it filled all the house where they were sitting.*
>
> *And there appeared unto them cloven tongues like as of fire, and it sat upon each of them.*
>
> *And they were all filled with the Holy Ghost, and began to speak with other tongues, as the Spirit gave them utterance.*

Again, we see here that 120 people were filled with the Holy Ghost, and they all began to speak with other tongues.

In these three instances–Acts 19, Acts 10, and Acts 2, we find three different events in three different places with three different groups of people, yet all of them had the exact same experience. Once they were filled with the Holy Spirit, they began to speak with other tongues. If this gift only manifested one time, there would be reason to wonder if this is available to every believer. But time and time again, we see this heavenly language come upon people who have received the Holy Spirit, and this manifestation has not changed since the time of the early church. Although people have mixed opinions on this topic, if you study the complete counsel of God on the subject, you can clearly see that being filled with the Holy Spirit and praying in other tongues is for today, and it is available for every believer.

CHAPTER

4

WHY
TONGUES

As a pastor, I do my best to help people see and understand the invaluable truths we find in the Word of God. Throughout my years of ministering, the phrase "why tongues" has surfaced often. Because I have experienced the value of praying in tongues in my own life, it has baffled me why people seem to have a difficult time grasping this truth. Clearly the enemy goes out of his way to deceive Christians into thinking that speaking in tongues is not applicable to their lives. Perhaps they use some of the Apostle Paul's instructions to the church at Corinth from I Corinthians 14 to convince themselves that speaking in other tongues is only appropriate in certain settings, and therefore they "excuse" themselves from praying in the Spirit at all. Regardless of a person's reason to not pray in tongues, there is a certain power available to every believer, and it will only be accessed by praying in other tongues.

Over the years, I have asked the Lord why there is so much confusion in the body of Christ regarding tongues and why many people seem to have such a difficult time understanding the purpose behind praying in tongues. In my quest for answers, I realized while we think it's about tongues, it is not; it's really about the power.

> **Acts 1:8 KJV,** ***But ye shall receive power, after that the Holy Ghost is come upon you: and you shall be witnesses unto me both in Jerusalem, and in all***

Whether is easier, to say, Thy sins be forgiven thee; or to say, Rise up and walk?

But that ye may know that the Son of man hath power upon earth to forgive sins, (He said unto the sick of the palsy,) I say unto thee, Arise, and take up thy couch, and go into thine house.

And immediately he rose up before them, and took up that whereon he lay, and departed to his own house, glorifying God.

And they were all amazed, and they glorified God, and were filled with fear,

And when they could not find by what way they might bring him in because of the multitude, they went upon the housetop, and let him down through the tiling with his couch into the midst before Jesus.

Here is a group of men who wanted to see this paralyzed man healed. However, because the room was so crowded, they could not even get him in the door. It makes me wonder just how many Pharisees and scribes were present, listening to Jesus teach! Because the friends of this paralyzed man could not find a way in, they took the roof off of the house and lowered him down to get to Jesus.

> Luke 5:20-26 KJV, *And when He saw their faith, He said unto him, Man, thy sins are forgiven thee.*
>
> *And the scribes and the Pharisees began to reason, saying, Who is this which speaketh blasphemies? Who can forgive sins, but God alone?*
>
> *But when Jesus perceived their thoughts, He answering said unto them, What reason ye in your hearts?*

to them through the Holy Spirit. The enemy never wants followers of Jesus to tap into and make use of this power. Let's look at a story in Luke 5 where we find Jesus teaching the Word to the Pharisees and scribes.

> Luke 5:17 KJV, ***And it came to pass on a certain day, as He was teaching, that there were Pharisees and doctors of the law sitting by, which were come out of every town of Galilee, and Judaea, and Jerusalem: and the power of the Lord was present to heal them.***

In this room, Jesus was surrounded by Pharisees and scribes who had come from numerous places, and the power of the Lord was present to heal them. Apparently, there were some Pharisees and doctors of the law in need of healing that were in that room. According to this verse, nobody else was mentioned as being a candidate for experiencing the power of the Lord.

> Luke 5:18-19 KJV, ***And, behold, men brought in a bed a man which was taken with a palsy: and they sought means to bring him in, and to lay him before Him.***

Judea, and in Samaria, and unto the uttermost part of the earth.

Notice in this verse that there is a promise of receiving power after the Holy Spirit came upon them. In Acts 2 we see this verse fulfilled when the Holy Spirit came and filled everyone that was gathered together, waiting for Him to come. With certainty they received the power they were promised, and they also began speaking with other tongues.

We are very familiar with natural power and what it can do in our lives. When you walk into a dark room and turn on a light switch, you're simply allowing power to flow to the lights that are installed. Can you imagine what life would look like without power? In the sanctuary of our church, we have multiple pieces of equipment that run on electrical power such as lights, microphones, sound boards, screens, cameras, etc. We could own the absolute best equipment, but if there was no power connected to the equipment, the equipment would serve absolutely no purpose. The equipment needs power to operate, and so it is in the life of the believer.

The enemy has done a masterful job of bringing confusion regarding the subject of other tongues so people become bewildered and fearful and confused just thinking about tongues. However, what the enemy is really after in the life of a believer in Christ is to rob them of the power available

What does it mean to be spirit filled?

In this story, did any of the people get healed for which the power of the Lord was present? No! The only person to get healed was a man who wasn't even in the room when the power of the Lord came into the room. Just think about all the people who could have received healing that day, but only one person took advantage of the power that was present. According to Jesus, it was the faith of this group of men that lowered the man through the roof, whereby the paralyzed man rose up off his bed and walked away healed.

There was power present in that room to heal, to bless, and to change lives. But none of those people benefited from it. They walked away in the exact same state they were in when they came, because they never took advantage of the power that was present.

There are far too many Christians today who have the exact same story. The power of the Lord is present in their lives, but because they have never received that power, they continue to live the same life day after day, week after week, month after month, year after year. They're living a powerless life, for no other reason than they just don't pursue the gift of the Holy Spirit and the power that is available to them.

Do you want to know how to tap into that power in you? It's by praying in other tongues. Tongues is the gift that God has given you to enable the power that is within you to be manifested. It is a private gift between you and the Father that manifests public power. By praying in other tongues, we can become the absolute best man or best woman that God created us to be.

There is a story in John chapter 4 that illustrates the purpose of praying in tongues so beautifully. Jesus had been on a long journey, and He came upon a well in which He wanted some water. He had no way to draw out the water. He began talking to a woman at the well and she asked Him, "What good is it to be sitting by a well filled with water if you don't have any way to draw out the water?"

Everything Jesus needed was right there to be refreshed, to restore His strength, and to give Him life. It was literally right there. The problem was that Jesus didn't have any way to draw out the water. If you had given Jesus a hammer, a remote control, or any other tool, it would not have helped Him. The only thing that could have helped Him was a bucket with a rope. If Jesus had this specific tool, He could have easily dipped down into the well and pulled up the water that He needed.

In the same way that there was only one tool that could draw water out of this well, so it is for those who have been filled with the Holy Spirit. The way we access all that we have been filled with by the

Spirit of God is this amazing gift (tool) called other tongues.

The Well Within You

Let's look a little deeper into all that is within you. When Jesus was still on the earth, He told His disciples that He would not always be with them, and that it would be okay because He would send something (someone) that was even better for them. Of course, He was referring to the Holy Spirit.

> John 14:16-17 (AMPC), ***And I will ask the Father, and He will give you another Comforter (Counselor, Helper, Intercessor, Advocate, Strengthener, and Standby) that He may remain with you forever,***
>
> *The Spirit of Truth,* ***Whom the world cannot receive, because it does not recognize Him. But you know and recognize Him, for He lives with you (constantly) and will be in you.***

Notice a couple of things...where does the Holy Spirit live? In you. What does that mean for you as a Spirit-filled Christian? Inside of you dwells the Comforter, the Counselor, the Helper, the Intercessor, the Advocate, the Strengthener, the Standby. In other words, all the counsel, wisdom, help, strength, prayer, power, and might you could ever need is already inside of you. And when you pray in the Holy Spirit, you are tapping into that well and accessing what is in you.

The question that the woman at the well asked Jesus is the same question I want to ask you. What good is it to have all the counsel, all the comfort, all the help, all the wisdom, all the prayer, all the strength, and all the might inside of you if you can't get it out? The good news is that you can draw it out by praying in other tongues.

In John 7:38-39, Jesus said,

> **John 7:38-39a KJV,** ***"He who believes in Me, as the Scripture said, 'From his innermost being will flow rivers of living water.'"***
>
> ***But this He spoke of the Holy Spirit…***

When you have the power of the Holy Spirit in you, and you pray in other tongues, it's like lowering a bucket to fill it up with rivers of living water. By doing this, you're tapping into all the power, prayer, faith, wisdom, comfort, counsel, strength, and help that's available in the Holy Spirit.

Changing Into Another Man

Many years ago, I had a dream, and I knew that it was a God-inspired dream. In the dream, I saw myself, but it wasn't me. It was a better version of me. To be honest, it shook me. I looked different physically, and I could tell by what I saw in the dream, that I was at a different level financially. However, the thing that stood out to me the most was the anointing on my words and the weight they carried. I saw myself speaking to a gentleman who at that time was not on my staff. (He later joined my staff.) We were on an airplane, and I walked up to him and placed my hand on his shoulder. As I began speaking to him, I could sense the anointing, and it was greater than anything that I had ever experienced before.

When I woke up from the dream I was alarmed because I saw me, but it wasn't me. Then the Lord spoke this to me, "There's a you in you, that's greater than the you, you see." Well, this statement is true for every single person. It speaks of our potential and who we could be. The difference for me at this moment is that I actually saw it, it was so real that it shook me.

After this happened, I went up to my study, shut the door, got on my knees, and asked the Lord, "What would it take for me to be that?" There were two things the Holy Spirit spoke to me. First, I was to continue to walk in forgiveness. Second, He told me that I needed to pray in the Spirit (other tongues) more. When He said that, I knew it was an area of my life that I needed to shore up and give more attention.

I was reminded of the story of King Saul. (I Samuel 9:3-4:7) Before he was anointed king of Israel, he was out one day looking for some of his father's donkeys that had wandered away. After failing to find the donkeys, the person he was with had the idea of going to see the prophet, Samuel, in order to learn where the donkeys were. Unbeknownst to them, as they were approaching Samuel, Samuel was actually approaching them. The day before, while Samuel was praying, the Lord told him about a man who would be coming to him, looking for some donkeys. The Lord told him when that happened, that He wanted Samuel to anoint him to be king of Israel.

Saul was shocked when he learned that Samuel was about to anoint him to be king. Bombarded with feelings of insecurity, Saul felt extremely inadequate and unqualified for the job. Not only was his tribe the least of all the tribes of Israel, but his family was the least family within that tribe. To top it all off, he was considered the least of his entire family. Truly Saul was the least likely to ever be king, but regardless of how Saul felt at that moment, God saw something in Saul that he couldn't see himself. Take a look at what transpired after Saul had been anointed by Samuel.

I Samuel 10:5b-7 MEV, ***And the Spirit of the Lord will come upon you, and you will prophesy with them, and you will be turned into another man.***

And it will be, when these signs are come unto you, that you will do as the occasion serves you; *for God is with you.*

Notice the progression in these two verses.
1. The Spirit of the Lord came upon Saul.
2. Saul prophesied with them (in other words, speaking with inspired utterance.)
3. Saul was turned into another man.
4. Saul would do as the occasion required.

At this moment, the Spirit of the Lord came upon Saul, regardless of how insecure or unqualified he felt. One of the most beautiful aspects of the Holy Spirit is the fact that our feelings have nothing to do with His ability in our lives. He was there to turn Saul into another man – a God man – so that Saul could accomplish what would be required of him as king. For a moment, Saul became that "God man." In fact, people around him couldn't believe that this was the Saul they knew because the man he became was so different. Unfortunately, he didn't stay that way. Saul lost what he had received by lightly esteeming the Spirit of God, the presence of God, and inspired utterance.

This progression is the perfect picture of what happens to born-again Christians when they are filled with the Holy Spirit. In life, we all have moments when the occasion requires something of us. But you can't properly do as the occasion demands until you are turned into another man or woman. And this can't happen until you speak with inspired utterance or other tongues. And you can't speak with inspired utterance until the Spirit of the Lord comes upon you.

Here's where we fall short – we try to do as the occasion demands without being turned into another man, and as a result, we fail. The reason we haven't been changed is because we haven't been giving enough time to speaking with inspired utterance, which is other tongues. Remember, when you are filled with the Holy Spirit, there is a river of living water on the inside of you, and you draw out that water by praying in other tongues.

Imagine how far King Saul could have gone in his life as a king had he given proper attention to what the Lord did for him that day. However, we see how quickly Saul's life unraveled because he lightly esteemed the God ordained supernatural flow in his life.

In the same way, you have the potential to rise higher and live a life so marked by God Himself, if you will consecrate yourself to a life that draws from the living well of water within you.

In Acts chapter 2 we see the time when Peter was turned into another man after the Holy Spirit was poured out upon Him. Just months before this, he was standing before a young girl, denying that he ever even knew Christ. (Matthew 26:69-75) That must have been an all-time low for Peter. After all the time of personally being with Jesus, Peter showed his worst self in that moment because of fear and insecurity.

However, that wasn't the end of Peter's story. Once the Spirit of the Lord came upon Peter, and he began speaking in other tongues, he was instantly turned into another man. The living waters within him came bursting forth as he testified to the people what had taken place in his life and what was taking place on the day of Pentecost. As a result, 3,000 people were saved that very day, and the book of Acts began. No longer was he easily shaken. He tapped into the power that had come by being filled with the Holy Spirit and praying in other tongues.

The You in You

Friend, I'm telling you, there's a you in you that's greater than the you, you see. The Holy Spirit sees that "you," and He is there to help you become exactly who God created you to be. Within you dwells all the power, all the strength, all the might, all the wisdom, and all the counsel you will ever need. It's not enough to just be filled with the Holy

Spirit. If you want to reach your highest potential and be the greatest version of yourself, it's going to take you tapping into the well within you by praying in other tongues. By doing so, you will draw out everything that is already within you.

> **Romans 8:26-27 ASV,** ***And in like manner the Spirit also helpeth our infirmity: for we know not how to pray as we ought; but the Spirit himself maketh intercession for us with groanings which cannot be uttered;***
>
> ***And he that searcheth the hearts knoweth what is the mind of the Spirit, because he maketh intercession for the saints according to the will of God.***

According to this verse, when we pray in the Holy Spirit, we make intercession according to the will of God, which means we pray according to the will of God. There is absolutely no greater fulfillment you can experience than being in the perfect will of God. Not only does the well within you contain all the power, wisdom, and direction you will ever need; it also contains the perfect will of God for your life. As you give yourself to praying in other tongues, you draw out the power, wisdom, and direction to live out the perfect will of God.

Several years ago I was talking to an individual who owns his own insurance agency. He had just stepped into a new season where it seemed that suddenly everything started clicking for him. So I asked him, "Are you doing anything different in your life?" He said, "A couple months ago, I heard you minister on praying in other tongues, and how it releases power, causing you to be a better version of yourself and changing you into another man. So I decided that on my way to work and on my way home from work, which is 15 minutes each way, I would just pray in an unknown tongue. This is the only thing I can tell that I'm doing differently."

Think about that – simply taking those 15 minutes each way, praying in other tongues, caused what he had been doing for years to suddenly take off. Why is that? Because when he started praying in other tongues, he began tapping into the power of God. That well of wisdom, counsel, and ability that is within him began coming out by leading his steps and helping him make wise decisions. No longer was he guessing about what to do; he was being directed and helped by the Holy Spirit within him.

What could your life look like if you begin drawing water out of the well within you? Where praying in tongues is concerned, it simply comes down to making it a priority in your life and disciplining yourself to pray. It's choosing to turn off sources of entertainment in the car on your way to and from work and praying in the Holy Spirit. It's choosing to wake up a few minutes earlier so you have time to set aside to pray in other tongues.

Have you ever heard of the rule of 100? This rule states that if you spend 100 hours a year, which is 18 minutes a day – in any discipline – you'll be better than 95% of the world in that discipline. I challenge you today to put this rule to the test and establish the discipline of praying in other tongues for at least 18 minutes every day. I truly believe that you will experience a noticeable difference in your life by praying 100 hours in the Holy Spirit over the course of one year. In fact, it will be so noticeable that you'll be encouraged and inspired to pray even more each day.

If there are things out of order in your life right now, know that as you give yourself to praying in tongues, those things will come back into order. If there is darkness in an area of your life, by praying in other tongues, you shine light in those dark places. By praying in other tongues, you take the limits off what you can do in your own strength, and you surrender to the power of God, allowing you to become the absolute best version of yourself that you can be.

CHAPTER 5

CONCLUSIONS

There has never been a time in history where the help of the Holy Spirit has been more needed in the lives of believers. I am so thankful for His help and involvement in my own life. I have learned that He sincerely desires to be the Helper that Jesus promised us – and this is for anyone who will receive Him.

I strongly encourage you today to pursue all that God has made available to you through this baptism in the Holy Spirit. Whether you have been filled with the Holy Spirit for many years or you have recently been baptized by the Holy Spirit, you'll never reach a point with Him where He has no more to give you. He is your ever-present help, regardless of what you need and where you are in life.

Baptism into Christ

If you don't have a personal relationship with Jesus, then being baptized into Christ is your first step towards eternal life and experiencing the greatest life on earth you can imagine. Without a doubt it is the most important decision you will ever make, and it's as easy as believing and praying the prayer below.

> *Dear Lord Jesus:*
> *Your Word says that if I confess with*
> *my mouth that Jesus is Lord and*
> *believe in my heart that God has*

raised Him from the dead, I shall be saved. (Romans 10:9)

Jesus, I believe in my heart and confess with my mouth that you were raised from the dead. I ask you now to be my Lord and Savior. I thank you for forgiving me of all my sins. I thank you that I now belong to you, and I am part of the family of God.

Friend, if you prayed that prayer for the first time, you are now a child of God, and you have sealed your place in Heaven. You just made the best decision of your life!

Baptism into Water

Have you been baptized in water? This outward demonstration of what has taken place on the inside of you will help you more than you realize. I encourage you to find a local church that you can join as you grow spiritually and ask to be water baptized!

Baptism in the Holy Spirit

If you have never been filled with the Holy Spirit, you can receive that gift right now! All you have to do is ask for it. In Luke 11:11-13, Jesus said, "Now suppose one of you fathers is asked by his son for a fish; he will not give him a snake instead of a fish, will he? Or if he is asked for an egg, he will not give him a scorpion, will he? If you then, being evil, know how to give good gifts to your children, **how much more will your heavenly Father give the Holy Spirit to those who ask Him?"** When you ask the Father for the baptism of the Holy Spirit, He will give it to you. Simply pray the prayer below.

> *Father:*
> *You told me in Luke 11:13 that if I ask for the Holy Spirit you would give Him to me. As Your child, I desire to be an instrument for Your Kingdom to manifest through my life. Would You fill me with this Spirit as You did for those in Acts? I desire to receive Your Promise of the Holy Spirit to those who believe.*
>
> *Jesus, my Savior and King, baptize me in the Holy Spirit so that the power of Your nature will work in me and transform me according to Your will. Holy Spirit, empower me and fill me to overflowing. I hold nothing back from You. Work Your gifts in me and through me, all of me, so that the*

Father's kingdom may be manifested in and through my life. I ask this in Jesus' mighty Name. Amen!

As soon as you pray that prayer, try to not speak in your native language. As you open your mouth, begin to speak out the utterances coming from your innermost being. I strongly encourage you to find a local church that can help you grow in your Spirit-filled life as you begin speaking in your heavenly language.

SHARE YOUR GOOD NEWS

If you prayed today to receive salvation or the infilling of the Holy Spirit, please contact our office. We rejoice with you, and we want to hear from you!

www.thelife.cc/prayer
or **email us at prayer@thelife.cc**.

❑ WORD OF LIFE

If you live near one of our campuses, please come visit us sometime soon. We would love to meet you! You can find our locations, service times, and information about Word of Life at **www.thelife.cc**.

We have many online resources available for you at **www.thelifeonline.cc**. You can find teachings on subjects like the baptism in the Holy Spirit, praying in the Spirit, healing, relationships, and much more.

AT THE AGE OF 19, JOEL SIMS BECAME THE LEAD PASTOR AT WORD OF LIFE CHURCH LOCATED IN JACKSON, MISSISSIPPI. He spent the next few years learning how to pastor the church his father and mother founded.

Now, over 20 years later, Word of Life is a thriving church that currentlys consists of four physical campuses and a large online presence. Joel's heart is to help pastors all over the world build strong churches as well as fund missionaries where they can fulfill all God has placed in their hearts.

Joel has been married to his wife, Peppi, for 18 years and they have 3 children: Reece, Boston, and Ben.